THE KING OF
THE DARK CHAMBER

THE MACMILLAN COMPANY
NEW YORK · BOSTON · CHICAGO · DALLAS
ATLANTA · SAN FRANCISCO

MACMILLAN & CO., LIMITED
LONDON · BOMBAY · CALCUTTA
MELBOURNE

THE MACMILLAN CO. OF CANADA, LTD.
TORONTO

THE KING

OF

THE DARK CHAMBER

BY

RABINDRANATH TAGORE

TRANSLATED INTO ENGLISH
BY THE AUTHOR

New York
THE MACMILLAN COMPANY
1914

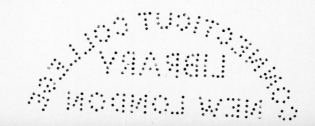

THE KING OF
THE DARK CHAMBER

THE KING OF THE DARK CHAMBER

I

A street. A few wayfarers, and a CITY GUARD

First Man

Ho, Sir!

City Guard

What do you want?

Second Man

Which way should we go? We are
strangers here. Please tell us which
street we should take.

City Guard

Where do you want to go?

Third Man

To where those big festivities are going to be held, you know. Which way do we go?

City Guard

One street is quite as good as another here. Any street will lead you there. Go straight ahead, and you cannot miss the place.

[Exit.

First Man

Just hear what the fool says: "Any street will lead you there!" Where, then, would be the sense of having so many streets?

Second Man

You needn't be so awfully put out at that, my man. A country is free to arrange its affairs in its own way.

As for roads in our country—well, they are as good as non-existent; narrow and crooked lanes, a labyrinth of ruts and tracks. Our King does not believe in open thoroughfares; he thinks that streets are just so many openings for his subjects to fly away from his kingdom. It is quite the contrary here; nobody stands in your way, nobody objects to your going elsewhere if you like to; and yet the people are far from deserting this kingdom. With such streets our country would certainly have been depopulated in no time.

First Man

My dear Janardan, I have always noticed that this is a great fault in your character.

Janardan

What is?

First Man

That you are always having a fling
at your country. How can you think
that open highways may be good for
a country? Look here, Kaundilya;
here is a man who actually believes
that open highways are the salvation
of a country.

Kaundilya

There is no need, Bhavadatta, of
my pointing out afresh that Janardan
is blessed with an intelligence which
is remarkably crooked, which is sure
to land him in danger some day. If
the King comes to hear of our worthy
friend, he will make it a pretty hard
job for him to find any one to do him
his funeral rites when he is dead.

Bhavadatta

One can't help feeling that life becomes a burden in this country; one

misses the joys of privacy in these streets — this jostling and brushing shoulders with strange people day and night makes one long for a bath.   And nobody can tell exactly *what* kind of people you are meeting with in these public roads—ugh!

Kaundilya

And it is Janardan who persuaded us to come to this precious country! We never had any second person like him in our family.   You knew my father, of course; he was a great man, a pious man if ever there was one. He spent his whole life within a circle of a radius of 49 cubits drawn with a rigid adherence to the injunctions of the scriptures, and never for a single day did he cross this circle. After his death a serious difficulty arose—how cremate him within the limits of the 49 cubits and yet outside

the house? At length the priests
decided that though we could not
go beyond the scriptural number, the
only way out of the difficulty was to
reverse the figure and make it 94
cubits; only thus could we cremate
him outside the house without violat-
ing the sacred books. My word, *that*
was strict observance! Ours is indeed
no common country.

Bhavadatta

And yet, though Janardan comes
from the very same soil, he thinks it
wise to declare that open highways
are best for a country.

Enter GRANDFATHER *with a band of boys*

Grandfather

Boys, we will have to vie with the
wild breeze of the south to-day—and

we are not going to be beaten. We
will sing till we have flooded all streets
with our mirth and song.

Song

The southern gate is unbarred. Come,
*   my spring, come!*
Thou wilt swing at the swing of my
*   heart, come, my spring, come!*
Come in the lisping leaves, in the youth-
*   ful surrender of flowers;*
Come in the flute songs and the wistful
*   sighs of the woodlands!*
Let your unfastened robe wildly flap in
*   the drunken wind!*
*   Come, my spring, come!*
*   [Exeunt.*

Enter a band of CITIZENS

First Citizen

After all, one cannot help wishing
that the King had allowed himself to

be seen at least this one day. What a great pity, to live in his kingdom and yet not to have seen him for a single day!

Second Citizen

If you only knew the real meaning of all this mystery! I could tell you if you would keep a secret.

First Citizen

My dear fellow, we both live in the same quarter of the town, but have you ever known me letting out any man's secret? Of course, that matter of your brother's finding a hidden fortune while digging for a well—well, you know well enough why I had to give it out. You know all the facts.

Second Citizen

Of course I know. And it is because I know that I ask, could you keep a secret if I tell you? It may mean ruination to us all, you know, if you once let it out.

Third Citizen

You are a nice man, after all, Virupaksha! Why are you so anxious to bring down a disaster which as yet only *may* happen? Who will be responsible for keeping your secret all his life?

Virupaksha

It is only because the topic came up —well, then, I shall not say anything. I am not the man to say things for nothing. You had yourself brought up the question that the King never showed himself; and I only remarked that it was not for nothing that the King shut himself up from the public gaze.

First Citizen

Pray do tell us why, Virupaksha.

Virupaksha

Of course I don't mind telling you—for we are all good friends, aren't we? There can be no harm. (*With a low voice.*) The King—is—hideous to look at, so he has made up his mind never to show himself to his subjects.

First Citizen

Ha! that's it! It must be so. We have always wondered . . . why, the mere sight of a King in all countries makes one's soul quake like an aspen leaf with fear; but why should *our* King never have been seen by any mortal soul? Even if he at least came out and consigned us all to the gibbet, we might be sure that our King was no hoax. After all, there is much in

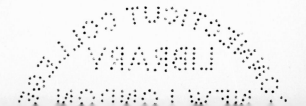

Virupaksha's explanation that sounds plausible enough.

Third Citizen

Not a bit—I don't believe in a syllable of it.

Virupaksha

What, Vishu, do you mean to say that I am a liar?

Vishu

I don't exactly mean that—but I cannot accept your theory. Excuse me, I cannot help if I seem a bit rude or churlish.

Virupaksha

Small wonder that you can't believe my words—you who think yourself sage enough to reject the opinions of your parents and superiors. How long do you think you could have stayed in this country if the King did not remain in hiding? You are no better than a flagrant heretic.

Vishu

My dear pillar of orthodoxy! Do you think any other King would have hesitated to cut off your tongue and make it food for dogs? And you have the face to say that our King is horrid to look at!

Virupaksha

Look here, Vishu, will you curb your tongue?

Vishu

It would be superfluous to point out whose tongue needs the curbing.

First Citizen

Hush, my dear friends—this looks rather bad. . . . It seems as if they are resolved to put me in danger as well. I am not going to be a party to all this.   [*Exit.*

Enter a number of men, dragging in GRANDFATHER, *in boisterous exuberance*

Second Citizen

Grandpa, something strikes me today . . .

Grandfather

What is it?

Second Citizen

This year every country has sent its people to our festival, but every one asks, "Everything is nice and beautiful—but where is your King?" and we do not know what to answer. That is the one big gap which cannot but make itself felt to every one in our country.

Grandfather

"Gap," do you say! Why, the whole country is all filled and crammed and packed with the King: and you call him a "gap"! Why, he has made every one of us a crowned King!

Sings

We are all Kings in the kingdom of our
    King.
Were it not so, how could we hope in our
    heart to meet him!
We do what we like, yet we do what he
    likes;
We are not bound with the chain of
    fear at the feet of a slave-owning
    King.
Were it not so, how could we hope in our
    heart to meet him!
Our King honours each one of us, thus
    honours his own very self.
No littleness can keep us shut up in its
    walls of untruth for aye.

*Were it not so, how could we have hope
        in our heart to meet him!*
*We struggle and dig our own path, thus
        reach his path at the end.*
*We can never get lost in the abyss of
        dark night.*
*Were it not so, how could we hope in our
        heart to meet him!*

Third Citizen

But, really, I cannot stand the absurd things people say about our King simply because he is not seen in public.

First Citizen

Just fancy! Any one libelling me can be punished, while nobody can stop the mouth of any rascal who chooses to slander the King.

Grandfather

The slander cannot touch the King.

With a mere breath you can blow out the flame which a lamp inherits from the sun, but if all the world blow upon the sun itself its effulgence remains undimmed and unimpaired as before.

Enter VISHVAVASU *and* VIRUPAKSHA

Vishu

Here's Grandfather! Look here, this man is going about telling everybody that our King does not come out because he is ugly.

Grandfather

But why does that make you angry, Vishu? *His* King must be ugly, because how else could Virupaksha possess such features in his kingdom? He fashions his King after the image of himself he sees in the mirror.

Virupaksha

Grandfather, I shall mention no names, but nobody would think of disbelieving the person who gave me the news.

Grandfather

Who could be a higher authority than yourself!

Virupaksha

But I could give you proofs . . .

First Citizen

The impudence of this fellow knows no bounds! Not content with spreading a ghastly rumour with an unabashed face, he offers to measure his lies with insolence!

Second Citizen

Why not make him measure his length on the ground?

Grandfather

Why so much heat, my friends? The poor fellow is going to have his own festive day by singing the ugliness of his King. Go along, Virupaksha, you will find plenty of people ready to believe you: may you be happy in their company.   [*Exeunt*.

Re-enter the party of FOREIGNERS

Bhavadatta

It strikes me, Kaundilya, that these people haven't got a King at all. They have somehow managed to keep the rumour afloat.

Kaundilya

You are right, I think. We all know that the supreme thing that strikes one's eye in any country is the King, who of course loses no opportunity of exhibiting himself.

Janardan

But look at the nice order and
regularity prevailing all over the place
—how do you explain it without a
King?

Bhavadatta

So this is the wisdom you have
arrived at by living so long under a
ruler! Where would be the necessity
of having a King if order and harmony
existed already?

Janardan

All these people have assembled
to rejoice at this festival. Do you
think they could come together like
this in a country of anarchy?

Bhavadatta

My dear Janardan, you are evading
the real issue, as usual. There can

be no question about the order and
regularity, and the festive rejoicing
too is plain enough: there is no difficulty so far. But where is the King?
Have you seen him? Just tell us
that.

Janardan

What I want to say is this: you
know from your experience that there
can be chaos and anarchy even if a
King be present: but what do we see
here?

Kaundilya

You are always coming back to your
quibbling. Why can you not give
a straight answer to Bhavadatta's
question—Have you, or have you not,
seen the King? Yes or no?

[*Exeunt.*

Enter a band of MEN, *singing*

Song

My beloved is ever in my heart
   That is why I see him everywhere,
He is in the pupils of my eyes
   That is why I see him everywhere.
I went far away to hear his own words,
   But, ah, it was vain!
When I came back I heard them
     In my own songs.
Who are you who seek him like a beggar
   from door to door!
Come to my heart and see his face in the
   tears of my eyes!

Enter HERALDS *and* ADVANCE GUARDS
of the KING

First Herald

Stand off! Get away from the
street, all of you!

First Citizen

Eh, man, who do you think you are? You weren't of course born with such lofty strides, my friend?— Why should we stand off, my dear sir? Why should we budge? Are we street dogs, or what?

Second Herald

Our King is coming this way.

Second Citizen

King? Which King?

First Herald

Our King, the King of this country.

First Citizen

What, is the fellow mad? Who- ever heard of our King coming out heralded by these vociferous gentry?

Second Herald

The King will no longer deny himself to his subjects. He is coming to command the festivities himself.

Second Citizen

Brother, is that so?

Second Herald

Look, his banner is flying over there.

Second Citizen

Ah, yes, that is a flag indeed.

Second Herald

Do you see the red *Kimshuk* flower painted on it?

Second Citizen

Yes, yes, it is the *Kimshuk* indeed! —what a bright scarlet flower!

First Herald

Well! do you believe us now?

Second Citizen

I never said I didn't. That fellow Kumbha started all this fuss. Did I say a word?

First Herald

Perhaps, though a pot-bellied man, he is quite empty inside; an empty vessel sounds most, you know.

Second Herald

Who is he? Is he any kinsman of yours?

Second Citizen

Not at all. He is just a cousin of our village chief's father-in-law, and he does not even live in the same part of our village with us.

Second Herald

Just so: he quite looks the seventh cousin of somebody's father-in-law, and his understanding appears also to bear the stamp of uncle-in-lawhood.

Kumbha

Alas, my friends, many a bitter sorrow has given my poor mind a twist before it has become like this. It is only the other day that a King came and paraded the streets, with as many titles in front of him as the drums that made the town hideous by their din. . . . What did I not do to serve and please him! I rained presents on him, I hung about him like a beggar—and in the end I found the strain on my resources too hard to bear. But what was the end of all that pomp and majesty? When people sought grants and presents from him, he could not somehow discover an auspicious day in the Calendar: though all days were red-letter days when *we* had to pay our taxes!

Second Herald

Do you mean to insinuate that our King is a bogus King like the one you have described?

First Herald

Mr. Uncle-in-law, I believe the time has come for you to say good-bye to Aunty-in-law.

Kumbha

Please, sirs, do not take any offence. I am a poor creature—my sincerest apologies, sirs: I will do anything to be excused. I am quite willing to move away as far as you like.

Second Herald

All right, come here and form a line. The King will come just now—we shall go and prepare the way for him.

[*They go out.*

Second Citizen

My dear Kumbha, your tongue will be your death one day.

Kumbha

Friend Madhav, it isn't my tongue, it is fate. When the bogus King appeared I never said a word, though that did not prevent my striking at my own feet with all the self-confidence of innocence. And now, when perhaps the real King has come, I simply must blurt out treason. It is fate, my dear friend!

Madhav

My faith is, to go on obeying the King—it does not matter whether he is a real one or a pretender. What do we know of Kings that we should judge them! It is like throwing stones in the dark—you are almost sure of hitting your mark. I go on obeying and acknowledging—if it is a real King, well and good: if not, what harm is there?

Kumbha

I should not have minded if the stones were nothing better than stones. But they are often precious things: here, as elsewhere, extravagance lands us in poverty, my friend.

Madhav

Look! There comes the King! Ah, a King indeed! What a figure, what a face! Whoever saw such beauty— lily-white, creamy-soft! What now, Kumbha? What do you think now?

Kumbha

He looks all right—yes, he may be the real King for all I know.

Madhav

He looks as if he were moulded and carved for kingship, a figure too exquisite and delicate for the common light of day.

Enter the "KING"

Madhav

Prosperity and victory attend thee, O King! We have been standing here to have a sight of thee since the early morning. Forget us not, your Majesty, in your favours.

Kumbha

The mystery deepens. I will go and call Grandfather.   [*Goes out.*

Enter another band of MEN

First Man

The King, the King! Come along, quick, the King is passing this way.

Second Man

Do not forget me, O King! I am Vivajadatta, the grandson of Udaya-datta of Kushalivastu. I came here at the first report of thy coming—I did not stop to hear what people were saying: all the loyalty in me went out towards thee, O Monarch, and brought me here.

Third Man

Rubbish! I came here earlier than you—before the cockcrow. Where were you then? O King, I am Bhad-rasena, of Vikramasthali. Deign to keep thy servant in thy memory!

King

I am much pleased with your loyalty and devotion.

Vivajadatta

Your Majesty, many are the griev-ances and complaints we have to make

to thee: to whom could we turn our
prayers so long, when we could not
approach thy august presence?

King

Your grievances will all be redressed.
                                    [*Exit.*

First Man

It won't do to lag behind, boys—
the King will lose sight of us if we get
mixed up with the mob.

Second Man

See there—look what that fool Nar-
ottam is doing! He has elbowed his
way through all of us and is now
sedulously fanning the King with a
palm leaf!

Madhav

Indeed! Well, well, the sheer audac-
ity of the man takes one's breath
away.

Second Man

We shall have to pitch the fellow out of that place—is he fit to stand beside the King?

Madhav

Do you imagine the King will not see through him? His loyalty is obviously a little too showy and profuse.

First Man

Nonsense! Kings can't scent hypocrites as we do—I should not be surprised if the King be taken in by that fool's strenuous fanning.

Enter KUMBHA *with* GRANDFATHER

Kumbha

I tell you—he has just passed by this street.

Grandfather

Is that a very infallible test of Kingship?

Kumbha

Oh no, he did not pass unobserved: not one or two men but hundreds and thousands on both sides of the street have seen him with their own eyes.

Grandfather

That is exactly what makes the whole affair suspicious. When ever has *our* King set out to dazzle the eyes of the people by pomp and pageantry? He is not the King to make such a thundering row over his progress through the country.

Kumbha

But he may just have chosen to do so on this important occasion: you cannot really tell.

Grandfather

Oh yes, you can! My King cherishes no weathercock fancy, no fantastic vein.

Kumbha

But, Grandfather, I wish I could only describe him! So soft, so delicate and exquisite like a waxen doll! As I looked on him, I yearned to shelter him from the sun, to protect him with my whole body.

Grandfather

Fool, O precious ass that you are! *My* King a waxen doll, and *you* to protect him!

Kumbha

But seriously, Grandpa, he is a superb god, a miracle of beauty: I do not find a single other figure in this vast assembly that can stand beside his peerless loveliness.

Grandfather

If my King chose to make himself shown, your eyes would not have noticed him. He would not stand out like that amongst others—he is one of the people, he mingles with the common populace.

Kumbha

But did I not tell you I saw his banner?

Grandfather

What did you see displayed on his banner?

Kumbha

It had a red *Kimshuk* flower painted on it—the bright and glittering scarlet dazzled my eyes.

Grandfather

My King has a thunderbolt within a lotus painted on his flag.

Kumbha

But every one is saying, the King is out in this festival: *every one.*

Grandfather

Why, so he is, of course: but he has no heralds, no army, no retinue, no music bands or lights to accompany him.

Kumbha

So none could recognise him in his incognito, it seems.

Grandfather

Perhaps there are a few that can.

Kumbha

And those that can recognise him— does the King grant them whatever they ask for?

Grandfather

But they never ask for anything. No beggar will ever know the King.

The greater beggar appears like the King to the eyes of the lesser beggar. O fool, the man that has come out to-day attired in crimson and gold to beg from you—it is him whom you are trumpeting as your King! . . . Ah, there comes my mad friend! Oh come, my brothers! we cannot spend the day in idle wrangling and prating —let us now have some mad frolic, some wild enjoyment!

Enter the MAD FRIEND, *who sings*

Do you smile, my friends? Do you laugh, my brothers? I roam in search of the golden stag! Ah yes, the fleet-foot vision that ever eludes me!

Oh, he flits and glimpses like a flash and then is gone, the untamed rover of the wilds! Approach him and he is afar in a trice, leaving a cloud of haze and dust before thy eyes!

Yet I roam in search of the golden stag, though I may never catch him in these wilds! Oh, I roam and wander through woods and fields and nameless lands like a restless vagabond, never caring to turn my back.

You all come and buy in the market-place and go back to your homes laden with goods and provisions: but me the wild winds of unscalable heights have touched and kissed— Oh, I know not when or where!

I have parted with my all to get what never has become mine! And yet think my moanings and my tears are for the things I thus have lost!

With a laugh and a song in my heart I have left all sorrow and grief far behind me: Oh, I roam and wander through woods and fields and nameless lands—never caring to turn my vagabond's back!

II

A Dark Chamber. QUEEN SUDARSHANA. *Her Maid of Honour,* SURANGAMA

Sudarshana

Light, light! Where is light? Will the lamp never be lighted in this chamber?

Surangama

My Queen, all your other rooms are lighted—will you never long to escape from the light into a dark room like this?

Sudarshana

But why should this room be kept dark?

Surangama

Because otherwise you would know neither light nor darkness.

Sudarshana

Living in this dark room you have grown to speak darkly and strangely— I cannot understand you, Surangama. But tell me, in what part of the palace is this chamber situated? I cannot make out either the entrance or the way out of this room.

Surangama

This room is placed deep down, in the very heart of the earth. The King has built this room specially for your sake.

Sudarshana

Why, he has no dearth of rooms— why need he have made this chamber of darkness specially for me?

Surangama

You can meet others in the lighted rooms: but only in this dark room can you meet your lord.

Sudarshana

No, no—I cannot live without light —I am restless in this stifling dark. Surangama, if you can bring a light into this room, I shall give you this necklace of mine.

Surangama

It is not in my power, O Queen. How can I bring light to a place which he would have kept always dark!

Sudarshana

Strange devotion! And yet, is it not true that the King punished your father?

Surangama

Yes, that is true. My father used to gamble. All the young men of the country used to gather at my father's house—and they used to drink and gamble.

Sudarshana

And when the King sent away your father in exile, did it not make you feel bitterly oppressed?

Surangama

Oh, it made me quite furious. I was on the road to ruin and destruction: when that path was closed for me, I seemed left without any support, without any succour or shelter. I raged and raved like a wild beast in a cage—how I wanted to tear every one to pieces in my powerless anger!

Sudarshana

But how did you get this devotion towards that same King?

Surangama

How can I tell? Perhaps I could rely and depend on him *because* he was so hard, so pitiless!

Sudarshana

When did this change of feeling take place?

Surangama

I could not tell you—I do not know that myself. A day came when all the rebel in me knew itself beaten, and then my whole nature bowed down in humble resignation on the dust of the earth. And then I saw . . . I saw that he was as matchless in beauty as in terror. Oh, I was saved, I was rescued.

Sudarshana

Tell me, Surangama, I implore you, won't you tell me what is the King like to look at? I have not seen him yet for a single day. He comes to me in darkness, and leaves me in this dark room again. How many people have I not asked—but they all return vague and dark answers—it seems to me that they all keep back something.

Surangama

To tell you the truth, Queen, I could not say well what he is like. No— he is not what men call handsome.

Sudarshana

You don't say so? Not handsome!

Surangama

No, my Queen, he is not handsome. To call him beautiful would be to say far too little about him.

Sudarshana

All your words are like that—dark, strange, and vague. I cannot understand what you mean.

Surangama

No, I will *not* call him handsome. And it is because he is not beautiful that he is so wonderful, so superb, so miraculous!

Sudarshana

I do not quite understand you—though I like to hear you talk about him. But I must see him at any cost. I do not even remember the day when I was married to him. I have heard mother say that a wise man came before my marriage and said, "He who will wed your daughter is without a second on this earth." How often have I asked her to describe his appearance to me, but she only answers vaguely, and says she cannot say—she saw him through a veil, faintly and obscurely. But if he is the best among men, how can I sit still without seeing him?

Surangama

Do you not feel a faint breeze blowing?

Sudarshana

A breeze? Where?

Surangama

Do you not smell a soft perfume?

Sudarshana

No, I don't.

Surangama

The large door has opened . . . he is coming; my King is coming in.

Sudarshana

How can you perceive when he comes?

Surangama

I cannot say: I seem to hear his footsteps in my own heart. Being his servant of this dark chamber, I have developed a sense—I can know and feel without seeing.

Sudarshana

Would that I had this sense too, Surangama!

Surangama

You will have it, O Queen . . . this sense will awaken in you one day. Your longing to have a sight of him makes you restless, and therefore all your mind is strained and warped in that direction. When you are past this state of feverish restlessness, everything will become quite easy.

Sudarshana

How is it that it is easy to you, who are a servant, and so difficult to me, the Queen?

Surangama

It is because I am a mere servant that no difficulty baulks me. On the first day, when he left this room to my care, saying, "Surangama, you will always keep this chamber ready for me: this is all your task," then I did not say, even in thought, "Oh, give me the work of those who keep the other rooms lighted." No, but as soon as I bent all my mind to my task, a power woke and grew within me, and mastered every part of me unopposed. . . . Oh, there he comes! . . . he is standing outside, before the door. Lord! O King!

Song outside

Open your door.   I am waiting.
The ferry of the light from the dawn to
*   the dark is done for the day,*
*   The evening star is up.*
Have you gathered your flowers, braided
*   your hair,*
*   And donned your white robe for the*
*   night?*
The cattle have come to their folds and
*   birds to their nests.*
The cross paths that run to all quarters
*   have merged into one in the dark.*
Open your door.   I am waiting.

Surangama

O King, who can keep thy own
doors shut against thee?   They are
not locked or bolted—they will swing
wide open if you only touch them with
thy fingers.   Wilt thou not even touch
them?   Wilt thou not enter unless I
go and open the doors?

Song

*At a breath you can remove my veils,
     my lord!*
*If I fall asleep on the dust and hear not
     your call, would you wait till I
     wake?*
*Would not the thunder of your chariot
     wheel make the earth tremble?*
*Would you not burst open the door and
     enter your own house unbidden?*

Then do you go, O Queen, and open
the door for him: he will not enter
otherwise.

Sudarshana

I do not see anything distinctly in
the dark—I do not know where the
doors are. You know everything here
—go and open the doors for me.

SURANGAMA *opens the door, bows to the
     KING, and goes out. The KING
     will remain invisible throughout
     this play.*

Sudarshana

Why do you not allow me to see you in the light?

King

So you want to see me in the midst of a thousand things in broad daylight! Why should I not be the only thing you can feel in this darkness?

Sudarshana

But I *must* see you—I am longing to have a sight of you.

King

You will not be able to bear the sight of me—it will only give you pain, poignant and overpowering.

Sudarshana

How can you say that I shall be unable to bear your sight? Oh, I can feel even in this dark how lovely and

wonderful you are: why should I be
afraid of you in the light? But tell
me, can you see me in the dark?

King

Yes, I can.

Sudarshana

What do you see?

King

I see that the darkness of the infinite
heavens, whirled into life and being
by the power of my love, has drawn
the light of a myriad stars into itself,
and incarnated itself in a form of flesh
and blood. And in that form, what
aeons of thought and striving, untold
yearnings of limitless skies, the count-
less gifts of unnumbered seasons!

Sudarshana

Am I so wonderful, so beautiful?
When I hear you speak so, my heart

swells with gladness and pride. But
how can I believe the wonderful things
you tell me? I cannot find them in
myself!

King

Your own mirror will not reflect
them—it lessens you, limits you, makes
you look small and insignificant. But
could you see yourself mirrored in my
own mind, how grand would you
appear! In my own heart you are
no longer the daily individual which
you think you are—you are verily my
second self.

Sudarshana

Oh, do show me for an instant how
to see with your eyes! Is there nothing at all like darkness to you? I
am afraid when I think of this. This
darkness which is to me real and
strong as death—is this simply nothing

to you? Then how can there be any
union at all between us, in a place
like this? No, no—it is impossible:
there is a barrier betwixt us two:
not here, no, not in this place. I
want to find you and see you where I
see trees and animals, birds and stones
and the earth——

King

Very well, you can try to find me—
but none will point me out to you.
You will have to recognise me, if you
can, yourself. And even if anybody
professes to show me to you, how can
you be sure he is speaking the truth?

Sudarshana

I shall know you; I shall recognise
you. I shall find you out among
a million men. I cannot be mistaken.

King

Very well, then, to-night, during the festival of the full moon of the spring, you will try to find me out from the high turret of my palace—search for me with your own eyes amongst the crowd of people.

Sudarshana

Wilt thou be there among them?

King

I shall show myself again and again, from every side of the crowd. Surangama!

Enter SURANGAMA

Surangama

What is thy pleasure, lord?

King

To-night is the full moon festival of the spring.

Surangama

What have I to do to-night?

King

To-day is a festive day, not a day of work.   The pleasure gardens are in their full bloom—you will join in my festivities there.

Surangama

I shall do as thou desirest, lord.

King

The Queen wants to see me to-night with her own eyes.

Surangama

Where will the Queen see you?

King

Where the music will play at its sweetest, where the air will be heavy with the dust of flowers—there in the pleasure grove of silver light and mellow gloom.

Surangama

What can be seen in the hide-and-seek of darkness and light? There the wind is wild and restless, everything is dance and swift movement—will it not puzzle the eyes?

King

The Queen is curious to search me out.

Surangama

Curiosity will have to come back baffled and in tears!

Song

Ah, they would fly away, the restless vagrant eyes, the wild birds of the forest!

*But the time of their surrender will come,
    their flights hither and thither will
    be ended when*
*The music of enchantment will pursue
    them and pierce their hearts.*
  *Alas, the wild birds would fly to the
    wilderness!*

III

Before the Pleasure Gardens. Enter AVANTI,
KOSHALA, KANCHI, *and other* KINGS

Avanti

Will the King of this place not
receive us?

Kanchi

What manner of governing a country
is this? The King is having a festival
in a forest, where even the meanest
and commonest people can have easy
access!

Koshala

We ought to have had a separate
place set apart and ready for our
reception.

Kanchi

If he has not prepared such a place yet, we shall compel him to have one erected for us.

Koshala

All this makes one naturally suspect if these people have really got any King at all—it looks as if an unfounded rumour has led us astray.

Avanti

It may be so with regard to the King, but the Queen Sudarshana of this place isn't at all an unfounded rumour.

Koshala

It is only for her sake that I have cared to come at all. I don't mind omitting to see one who never makes himself visible, but it would be a stupid mistake if we were to go away without a sight of one who is eminently worth a visit.

Kanchi

Let us make some definite plan, then.

Avanti

A plan is an excellent thing, so long as you are not yourself entangled in it.

Kanchi

Hang it, who are these vermin swarming this way? Here! who are you?

Enter GRANDFATHER *and the boys*

Grandfather

We are the Jolly Band of Have-Nothings.

Avanti

The introduction was superfluous. But you will take yourselves away a little further and leave us in peace.

Grandfather

We never suffer from a want of space: we can afford to give you as wide a berth as you like. What little suffices for us is never the bone of contention between any rival claimants. Is not that so, my little friends?

[*They sing.*

Song

We have nothing, indeed we have nothing
at all!
    We sing merrily fol de rol de rol!
Some build high walls of their houses
    On the bog of the sands of gold.
We stand before them and sing
        Fol de rol de rol.
Pickpockets hover about us
    And honour us with covetous glances.
We shake our empty pockets and sing
        Fol de rol de rol.

When death, the old hag, steals to our
    doors
We snap our fingers at her face,
And we sing in a chorus with gay
    flourishes
        Fol de rol de rol.

Kanchi

Look over there, Koshala, who are those coming this way? A pantomime? Somebody is out masquerading as a King.

Koshala

The King of this place may tolerate all this tomfoolery, but we won't.

Avanti

He is perhaps some rural chief.

Enter GUARDS *on foot*

Kanchi

What country does your King come from?

First Soldier

He is the King of this country. He
is going to command the festivities.

                              [*They go out.*

Koshala

What! The King of this country
come out for the festivities!

Avanti

Indeed! We shall then have to
return with a sight of him only—
leaving the delectable Queen unseen.

Kanchi

Do you really think that fellow
spoke the truth? Anybody can pass
himself off as the King of this kingless
country. Can you not see that the
man looks like a dressed-up King—
much too over-dressed?

Avanti

But he looks handsome—his appearance is not without a certain pleasing attractiveness.

Kanchi

He may be pleasing to your eye, but if you look at him closely enough there can be no mistaking him. You will see how I expose him before you all.

Enter the trumped-up "KING."

"King"

Welcome, princes, to our kingdom! I trust your reception has been properly looked after by my officials?

Kings (with feigned courtesy)

Oh yes—nothing was lacking in the reception.

Kanchi

If there was any shortcoming at all, it has been made up by the honour of our sight of your Majesty.

"King"

We do not show ourselves to the general public, but your great devotion and loyalty to us has made it a pleasure for us not to deny ourselves to you.

Kanchi

It is truly hard for us, your Majesty, to bear the weight of your gracious favours.

"King"

We are afraid we shall not be able to stop here long.

Kanchi

I have thought so, already: you do not quite look up to it.

"King"

In the meantime if you have any favours to ask of us——

Kanchi

We have: but we would like to speak a little more in private.

"King" (*to his attendants*)

Retire a little from our presence. (*They retire.*) Now you can express your desires without any reserve.

Kanchi

There will be no reserve on our part —our only fear is that you might think restraint necessary for yourself.

"King"

Oh no, you need have no scruples on that score.

Kanchi

Come, then, do us honage by placing your head on the ground before us.

"King"

It seems my servants have distributed the Varuni spirits too liberally in the reception camps.

Kanchi

False pretender, it is you who are suffering from an overdose of arrogant spirits. Your head will soon kiss the dust.

"King"

Princes, these heavy jokes are not worthy of a king.

Kanchi

Those who will jest properly with you are near at hand. General!

"King"

No more, I entreat you. I can see plainly I owe homage to you all. The head is bowing down of itself—there is no need for the application of any sharp methods to lay it low. So here I do my obeisance to you all. If you kindly allow me to escape I shall not inflict my presence long on you.

Kanchi

Why should you escape? We will make you king of this place—let us carry our joke to its legitimate finish. Have you got any following?

"King"

I have. Every one who sees me in the streets flocks after me. When I had a meagre retinue at first every one regarded me with suspicion, but now with the increasing crowd their doubts are waning and dissolving. The crowd is being hypnotised by its own magnitude. I have not got to do anything now.

Kanchi

That's excellent! From this moment we all promise to help and
stand by you. But you will have to
do us one service in return.

"King"

Your commands and the crown you
are putting on my head will be equally
binding and sacred to me.

Kanchi

At present we want nothing more
than a sight of the Queen Sudarshana.
You will have to see to this.

"King"

I shall spare no pains for that.

Kanchi

We cannot put much faith on your
pains—you will be solely directed by

our instructions.   But now you can go and join the festivities in the royal arbour with all possible splendour and magnificence.   [*They go out.*

Enter GRANDFATHER *and a band of people*

First Citizen

Grandfather, I cannot help saying— yes, and repeating it five hundred times—that our King is a perfect fraud.

Grandfather

Why only five hundred times? There is no need to practise such heroic self-control—you can say it five thousand times if that adds to your pleasure.

Second Citizen

But you cannot keep up a dead lie forever.

Grandfather

It has made me alive, my friend.

Third Citizen

We shall proclaim to the whole world that our King is a lie, the merest and emptiest shadow!

First Citizen

We shall all shout from our house-tops that we have no King—let him do whatever he likes if he exists.

Grandfather

He will do nothing at all.

Second Citizen

My son died untimely at twenty-five of raging fever in seven days. Could such a calamity befall me under the rule of a virtuous King?

Grandfather

But you still have got two sons left: while I have lost all my five children one after another.

Third Citizen

What do you say now?

Grandfather

What then? Shall I lose my King too because I have lost my children? Don't take me for such a big fool as that.

First Citizen

It is a fine thing to argue whether there is a King or not when one is simply starving for want of food! Will the King save us?

Grandfather

Brother, you are right. But why not *find* the King who owns all the food?   You certainly will not find by your wailings at home.

Second Citizen

Look at the justice of our King! That Bhadrasen—you know what a touching sight he is when he is speaking of his King—the sentimental idiot! He is reduced to such a state of penury that even the bats that infest his house find it a too uncomfortable place.

Grandfather

Why, look at me! I am toiling and slaving night and day for my King, but I have not yet received so much as a brass farthing for my pains.

Third Citizen

Now, what do you think of that?

Grandfather

What should I think? Does any
one reward his friends? Go, my friends,
and say if you like that our King exists
nowhere. That is also a part of our
ceremony in celebrating this festival.

IV

Turret of the Royal Palace. SUDARSHANA *and
her friend* ROHINI

Sudarshana

You may make mistakes, Rohini,
but I cannot be mistaken: am I not
the Queen? That, of course, must
be my King.

Rohini

He who has conferred such high
honour upon you cannot be long in
showing himself to you.

Sudarshana

His very form makes me restless
like a caged bird. Did you try well
to ascertain who he is?

Rohini

Yes, I did. Every one I asked said that he was the King.

Sudarshana

What country is he the King of?

Rohini

Our country, King of this land.

Sudarshana

Are you sure that you are speaking of him who has a sunshade made of flowers held over his head?

Rohini

The same: he whose flag has the *Kimshuk* flower painted on it.

Sudarshana

I recognised him at once, of course, but it is you who had your doubts.

Rohini

We are apt to make mistakes, my Queen, and we are afraid to offend you in case we are wrong.

Sudarshana

Would that Surangama were here! There would remain no room for doubt then.

Rohini

Do you think her cleverer than any of us?

Sudarshana

Oh no, but she would recognise him instantly.

Rohini

I cannot believe that she would. She merely pretends to know him. There is none to test her knowledge if she professes to know the King. If we were as shameless as she is, it would not have been difficult for us to boast about our acquaintance with the King.

Sudarshana

But no, she never boasts.

Rohini

It is pure affectation, the whole of it: which often goes a longer way than open boasting. She is up to all manner of tricks: that is why we could never like her.

Sudarshana

But whatever you may say, I should have liked to ask her if she were here.

Rohini

Very well, Queen. I shall bring her here. She must be lucky if she is indispensable for the Queen to know the King.

Sudarshana

Oh no—it isn't for that—but I would like to hear it said by every one.

Rohini

Is not every one saying it? Why, just listen, the acclamations of the people mount up even to this height!

Sudarshana

Then do one thing: put these flowers on a lotus leaf, and take them to him.

Rohini

And what am I to say if he asks who sends them?

Sudarshana

You will not have to say anything— he will know. He thought that I would not be able to recognise him: I cannot let him off without showing that I have found him out.

[ROHINI *goes out with the flowers.*

Sudarshana

My heart is all a-quiver and restless to-night: I have never felt like this before. The white, silver light of the full moon is flooding the heavens and brimming over on every side like the bubbling foam of wine. . . . It seizes on me like a yearning, like a mantling intoxication. Here, who is here?

Enter a SERVANT

Servant

What is your pleasure, your Majesty?

Sudarshana

Do you see those festive boys singing and moving through the alleys and avenues of the mango trees? Call them hither, bring them to me: I want to hear them sing.

[SERVANT *goes out and enters with the boys.*

Come, living emblems of youthful spring, begin your festive song! All my mind and body is song and music to-night—but the ineffable melody escapes my tongue: do you then sing for my sake!

Song

My sorrow is sweet to me in this spring night.

My pain smites at the chords of my love and softly sings.

Visions take birth from my yearning eyes and flit in the moonlit sky.

The smells from the depths of the woodlands have lost their way in my dreams.

Words come in whispers to my ears, I know not from where,

And bells in my anklets tremble and jingle in time with my heart thrills.

Sudarshana

Enough, enough—I cannot bear it

any more! Your song has filled my eyes with tears. . . . A fancy comes to me—that desire can never attain its object—it need never attain it. What sweet hermit of the woods has taught you this song? Oh that my eyes could see him whose song my ears have heard! Oh, how I wish—I wish I could wander rapt and lovely in the thick woodland arbours of the heart! Dear boys of the hermitage! how shall I reward you? This necklace is but made of jewels, hard stones—its hardness will give you pain—I have got nothing like the garlands of flowers you have on.

[The boys bow and go out.

Enter ROHINI

Sudarshana

I have not done well—I have not done well, Rohini. I feel ashamed to

ask you what happened. I have just
realised that no hand can really give
the greatest of gifts. Still, let me
hear all.

Rohini

When I gave the King those flowers,
he did not appear to understand anything.

Sudarshana

You don't say so? He did not
understand——!

Rohini

No; he sat there like a doll, without
uttering a single word. I think he
did not want to show that he under-
stood nothing, so he just held his
tongue.

Sudarshana

Fie on me! My shamelessness has
been justly punished. Why did you
not bring back my flowers?

Rohini

How could I? The King of Kanchi,
a very clever man, who was sitting by
him, took in everything at a glance,
and he just smiled a bit and said,
"Emperor, the Queen Sudarshana
sends your Majesty her greetings with
these blossoms—the blossoms that be-
long to the God of Love, the friend of
Spring." The King seemed to awake
with a start, and said, "This is the
crown of all my regal glory to-night."
I was coming back, all out of counte-
nance, when the King of Kanchi took
off this necklace of jewels from the
King's person, and said to me, "Friend,
the King's garland gives itself up to
you, in return for the happy fortune
you have brought."

Sudarshana

What, Kanchi had to make the
King understand all this! Woe is

me, to-night's festival has opened wide
for me the doors of ignominy and
shame! What else could I expect?
Leave me alone, Rohini; I want soli-
tude for a time. (ROHINI *goes out.*)
A great blow has shattered my pride
to atoms to-day, and yet . . . I cannot efface from my mind that beautiful,
fascinating figure! No pride is left
me—I am beaten, vanquished, utterly
helpless. . . . I cannot even turn
away from him. Oh, how the wish
comes back to me again and again—
to ask that garland of Rohini! But
what would she think! Rohini!

Enter ROHINI

Rohini

What is your wish?

Sudarshana

What reward do you deserve for
your services to-day?

Rohini

Nothing from you—but I had my reward from the King as it should be.

Sudarshana

That is no free gift, but an extortion, of reward. I do not like to see you put on what was given in so indifferent a manner. Take it off— I give you my bracelets if you leave it here. Take these bracelets, and go now. (ROHINI *goes out*.) Another defeat! I should have thrown this necklace away,—but I could not! It is pricking me as if it were a garland of thorns—but I cannot throw it away. This is what the god of the festival has brought me to-night—this necklace of ignominy and shame!

V

Grandfather

Have you had enough of it, friends?

First Man

Oh, more than that, Grandpa. Just see, they have made me red all over. None has escaped.[1]

Grandfather

No? Did they throw the red dust on the Kings too?

---

[1] During the spring festival in India people throw red powder on each other. In this play this red powder has been taken to be the symbol of the passion of love.

Second Man

But who could approach them? They were all secure inside the enclosures.

Grandfather

So they have escaped you! Could you not throw the least bit of colour on them? You should have forced your way there.

Third Man

My dear old man, they have a different sort of red specially to themselves. Their eyes are red: the turbans of their guards and retinue are red too. And the latter flourished their swords about so much that a little more nearness on our part would have meant a lavish display of the fundamental red colour.

Grandfather

Well done, friends—always keep

them at a distance. They are the exiles of the Earth—and we have got to keep them so.

Third Man

I am going home, Grandpa; it is past midnight. [*Goes out.*

Enter a BAND *of* SINGERS, *singing.*

All blacks and whites have lost their distinction
And have become red—red as the tinge of your feet.
Red is my bodice and red are my dreams,
My heart sways and trembles like a red lotus.

Grandfather

Excellent, my friends, splendid! So you had a really enjoyable time!

Singers

Oh, grand! Everything was red, red! Only the moon in the sky gave us the slip—it remained white.

Grandfather

He only looks so innocent from the outside. If you had only taken off his white disguise, you would have seen his trickery. I have been watching what red colours he is throwing on the Earth to-night. And yet, fancy his remaining white and colourless all the while!

Song

With you is my game, love, my love!
My heart is mad, it will never own defeat,
Do you think you will escape stainless yourself reddening me with red powder?

*Could I not colour your robe with the
    red pollens of the blossom of my
    heart?*   [*They go out.*

*Enter the "*KING*" and* KANCHI.

Kanchi

You must do exactly as I have told
you. Let there be no mistake of any
kind.

"King"

There shall be no mistake.

Kanchi

The Queen Sudarshana's mansions
are in the . . .

"King"

Yes, sire, I have seen the place
well.

Kanchi

What you have got to do is to

set fire to the garden, and then you will take advantage of the bustle and confusion to accomplish your object straightway.

"King"

I shall remember.

Kanchi

Look here, Sir Pretender, I cannot help thinking that a needless fear is troubling us—there is really no King in this country.

"King"

My sole aim is to rid this country of this anarchy. Your common man cannot live without a King, whether a real one or a fraud! Anarchy is always a source of danger.

Kanchi

Pious benefactor of the people, your

wonderful self-sacrifice should really be an example to all of us. I am thinking of doing this extraordinary service to the people myself.

[*They go out.*

VI

Rohini

What is the matter? I cannot make out what is all this! (*To the gardeners.*) Where are you all going away in such a hurry?

First Gardener

We are going out of the garden.

Rohini

Where?

Second Gardener

We do not know where—the King has called us.

Rohini

Why, the King is in the garden.
Which King has called you?

First Gardener

We cannot say.

Second Gardener

The King we have been serving all
our life, of course.

Rohini

Will you all go?

First Gardener

Yes, all—we have to go instantly.
Otherwise we might get into trouble.
[*They go out.*

Rohini

I cannot understand their words.
. . . I am afraid. They are scamper-
ing off like wild animals that fly just

before the bank of a river breaks down into the water.

Enter KING OF KOSHALA

Koshala

Rohini, do you know where your King and Kanchi have gone?

Rohini

They are somewhere in the garden, but I could not tell you where.

Koshala

I cannot really understand their intentions. I have not done well to put my trust in Kanchi.   [*Exit.*

Rohini

What is this dark affair going on amongst these kings? Something dreadful is going to happen soon. Shall I too be drawn into this affair?

Enter AVANTI

Avanti

Rohini, do you know where the other princes are?

Rohini

It is difficult to say which of them is where. The King of Koshala just passed by in this direction.

Avanti

I am not thinking of Koshala. Where are your King and Kanchi?

Rohini

I have not seen them for a long time.

Avanti

Kanchi is always avoiding us. He is certainly planning to deceive us all. I have not done well to put my hand in this imbroglio. Friend, could you kindly tell me any way out of this garden?

Rohini

I have none.

Avanti

Is there no man here who will show me the way out?

Rohini

The servants have all left the garden.

Avanti

Why did they do so?

Rohini

I could not exactly understand what they meant. They said the King had commanded them to leave the garden at once.

Avanti

King? Which King?

Rohini

They could not say exactly.

Avanti

This does not sound well. I shall have to find a way out at any cost. I cannot stay here a single moment more.   [*Goes out hurriedly.*

Rohini

Where shall I find the King? When I gave him the flowers the Queen had sent, he did not seem much interested in me at the time; but ever since that hour he has been showering gifts and presents on me. This causeless generosity makes me more afraid. . . . Where are the birds flying at such an hour of the night? What has frightened them all on a sudden? This is not the usual time of their flight, certainly. . . . Why is the

Queen's pet deer running that way? Chapata! Chapata! She does not even hear my call. I have never seen a night like this! The horizon on every side suddenly becomes red, like a madman's eye! The sun seems to be setting at this untimely hour on all sides at the same time. What madness of the Almighty is this! . . . Oh, I am frightened! . . . Where shall I find the King?

VII

At the Door of the QUEEN's *Palace*

"King"

What is this you have done, Kanchi?

Kanchi

I wanted to fire only this part of the garden near the palace. I had no idea that it would spread so quickly on all sides. Tell me, quick, the way out of this garden.

"King"

I can tell you nothing about it. Those who brought us here have all fled away.

Kanchi

You are a native of this country—you must know the way.

"King"

I have never entered these inner royal gardens before.

Kanchi

I won't hear of it—you must show me the way, or I shall split you into halves.

"King"

You may take my life by that means, but it would be a very precarious method of finding the way out of this garden.

Kanchi

Why were you, then, going about saying that you were the King of this country?

"*King*"

I am not the King—I am not the King. (*Throwing himself on the ground with folded hands.*) Where art thou, my King? Save me, oh, save me! I am a rebel—punish me, but do not kill me!

Kanchi

What is the use of shouting and cringing to the empty air? It is a much better way of spending the time to search for the way.

"*King*"

I shall lie down here—I shall not move an inch. Come what will, I shall not complain.

Kanchi

I will not allow all this nonsense. If I am to be burnt to death, you will be my companion to the very end.

From the Outside

Oh, save us, save us, our King!
The fire is on all sides of us!

Kanchi

Fool, get up, lose no more time.

Sudarshana (*entering*)

King, O my King! save me, save
me from death! I am surrounded
by fire.

"King"

Who is the King? I am no King.

Sudarshana

You are not the King?

"King"

No, I am a hypocrite, I am a
scoundrel. (*Flinging his crown on
the ground.*) Let my deception and
hypocrisy be shattered into dust!

[*Goes out with* KANCHI.

Sudarshana

No King! He is not the King? Then, O thou God of fire, burn me, reduce me to ashes! I shall throw myself into thy hands, O thou great purifier; burn to ashes my shame, my longing, my desire.

Rohini (entering)

Queen, where are you going? All your inner chambers are shrouded in raging fire—do you not enter there.

Sudarshana

Yes! I will enter those burning chambers! It is the fire of my death!
[*Enters the Palace.*

VIII

The Dark Room.   The KING *and* SUDARSHANA

King

Do not be afraid—you have no
cause for fear.   The fire will not reach
this room.

Sudarshana

I have no fear—but oh, shame has
accompanied me like a raging fire.
My face, my eyes, my heart, every
part of my body is being scorched and
burnt by its flames.

King

It will be some time before you get
over this burning.

Sudarshana

This fire will never cease—will never cease!

King

Do not be despondent, Queen!

Sudarshana

O King, I shall not hide anything from you. . . . I have another's garland round my neck.

King

That garland, too, is mine—how else could he get it? He stole it from my room.

Sudarshana

But it is *his* gift to me: yet I could not fling this garland away! When the fire came roaring on all sides of me, I thought of throwing this garland into the fire. But no, I could not.

My mind whispered, "Let that garland be on you in your death." . . . What fire is this, O King, into which I, who had come out to see you, leaped like a moth that cannot resist the flame? What a pain is this, oh, what agony! The fire keeps burning as fiercely as ever, but I go on living within its flames!

King

But you have seen me at last—your desire has been fulfilled.

Sudarshana

But did I seek to see you in the midst of this fearful doom? I know not what I saw, but my heart is still beating fast with fear.

King

What did you see?

Sudarshana

Terrible,—oh, it was terrible! I am afraid even to think of it again. Black, black—oh, thou art black like the everlasting night! I only looked on thee for one dreadful instant. The blaze of the fire fell on your features— you looked like the awful night when a comet swings fearfully into our ken —oh, then I closed my eyes—I could not look on you any more. Black as the threatening storm-cloud, black as the shoreless sea with the spectral red tint of twilight on its tumultuous waves!

King

Have I not told you before that one cannot bear my sight unless one is already prepared for me? One would want to run away from me to the ends of the earth. Have I not seen this times without number? That is why

I wanted to reveal myself to you slowly and gradually, not all too sudden.

Sudarshana

But sin came and destroyed all your hopes—the very possibility of a union with you has now become unthinkable to me.

King

It will be possible in time, my Queen. The utter and bleak blackness that has to-day shaken you to your soul with fear will one day be your solace and salvation. What else can my love exist for?

Sudarshana

It cannot be, it is not possible. What will *your* love only do? *My* love has now turned away from you. Beauty has cast its spell on me—

this frenzy, this intoxication will never leave me—it has dazzled and fired my eyes, it has thrown its golden glamour over my very dreams! I have told you all now—punish me as you like.

King

The punishment has already begun.

Sudarshana

But if you do not cast me off. I will leave you——

King

You have the utmost liberty to do as you like.

Sudarshana

I cannot bear your presence! My heart is angry at you. Why did you —but what have you done to me? . . . Why are you like this? Why did they tell me you were fair and handsome? Thou art black, black as night

—I shall never, I can never, like you. I have seen what I love—it is soft as cream, delicate as the *shirisha* flower, beautiful as a butterfly.

King

It is false as a mirage, empty as a bubble.

Sudarshana

Let it be——but I cannot stand near you—I simply cannot! I must fly away from here. Union with you, it cannot be possible! It cannot be anything but a false union—my mind must inevitably turn away from you.

King

Will you not even try a little?

Sudarshana

I have been trying since yesterday —but the more I try, the more rebellious does my heart become. If I stay with you I shall constantly be pursued and hounded by the thought that I am impure, that I am false and faithless.

King

Well then, you can go as far from me as you like.

Sudarshana

I cannot fly away from you—just because you do not prevent my going. Why do you not hold me back, hold me by the hair, saying, "You shall not go"? Why do you not strike me? Oh, punish me, strike me, beat me with violent hands! But your unresisting silence makes me wild—oh, I cannot bear it!

King

How do you think that I am really silent? How do you know that I am not trying to keep you back?

Sudarshana

Oh, no, no!—I cannot bear this—
tell me aloud, command me with
the voice of thunder, compel me with
words that will drown everything else
in my ears—do not let me off so easily,
so mildly!

King

I shall leave you free, but why
should I let you break away from me?

Sudarshana

You will not let me?   Well then,
I must go!

King

Go then!

Sudarshana

Then I am not to blame at all.
You could have held me back by
force, but you did not! You have
not hindered me—and now I shall go

away.   Command your sentinels to prevent my going.

King

No one will stand in your way. You can go as free as the broken storm-cloud driven by the tempest.

Sudarshana

I can resist no more—something in me is impelling me forward—I am breaking away from my anchor! Perhaps I shall sink, but I shall return no more.   [*She rushes out.*

Enter SURANGAMA, *who sings*

Surangama

What will of thine is this that sends me afar! Again shall I come back at thy feet from all my wanderings.

It is thy love that feigns this neglect —thy caressing hands are pushing me away—to draw me back to thy arms again! O my King, what is this game that thou art playing throughout thy kingdom?

SUDARSHANA (*re-entering*)

King, O King!

Surangama

He has gone away.

Sudarshana

Gone away? Well then, . . . then he has cast me off for good! I have come back, but he could not wait a single instant for me! Very well, then, I am now perfectly free. Surangama, did he ask you to keep me back?

Surangama

No, he said nothing.

Sudarshana

Why should he say anything? Why should he care for me? . . . I am then free, perfectly free. But, Surangama, I wanted to ask one thing of the King, but could not utter it in his presence. Tell me if he has punished the prisoners with death.

Surangama

Death? My King never punishes with death.

Sudarshana

What has he done to them, then?

Surangama

He has set them at liberty. Kanchi has acknowledged his defeat and gone back to his kingdom.

Sudarshana

Ah, what a relief!

Surangama

My Queen, I have one prayer to make to you.

Sudarshana

You will not have to utter your prayer in words, Surangama. Whatever jewellery and ornaments the King gave me, I leave to you—I am not worthy to wear them now.

Surangama

No, I do not want them, my Queen. My master has never given me any ornaments to wear—my unadorned plainness is good enough for me. He has not given me anything of which I can boast before people.

Sudarshana

What do you want of me then?

Surangama

I too shall go with you, my Queen.

Sudarshana

Consider what you are saying; you are wanting to leave your master. What a prayer for you to make!

Surangama

I shall not go far from him—when you are going out unguarded he will be with you, close by your side.

Sudarshana

You are talking nonsense, my child. I wanted to take Rohini with me, but she would not come. What gives you courage enough to wish to come with me?

Surangama

I have got neither courage nor strength. But I shall go—courage will come of itself, and strength too will come.

Sudarshana

No, I cannot take you with me;

your presence will constantly remind me of my shame; I shall not be able to endure that.

Surangama

O my Queen, I have made all your good and all your evil my own as well; will you treat me as a stranger still? I must go with you.

IX

The KING OF KANYA KUBJA, *father of* SUDAR-
SHANA, *and his* MINISTER

King of Kanya Kubja

I heard everything before her arrival.

Minister

The princess is waiting alone outside the city gates on the bank of the river. Shall I send people to welcome her home?

King of Kanya Kubja

What! She who has faithlessly left her husband—do you propose trumpeting her infamy and shame to

128

every one by getting up a show for her?

Minister

Shall I then make arrangements for her residence at the palace?

King of Kanya Kubja

You will do nothing of the sort. She has left her place as the Empress of her own accord—here she will have to work as a maid-servant if she wants to stay in my house.

Minister

It will be hard and bitter to her, Your Highness.

King of Kanya Kubja

If I seek to save her from her sufferings, then I am not worthy to be her father.

Minister

I shall arrange everything as you wish, Your Highness.

King of Kanya Kubja

Let it be kept a secret that she is my daughter; otherwise we shall all be in an awful trouble.

Minister

Why do you fear such disaster, Your Highness?

King of Kanya Kubja

When woman swerves from the right path, then she appears fraught with the direst calamity. You do not know with what deadly fear this daughter of mine has inspired me— she is coming to my home laden with peril and danger.

X

Inner Apartments of the Palace. SUDARSHANA
and SURANGAMA

Sudarshana

Go away from me, Surangama! A
deadly anger rages within me—I cannot bear anybody—it makes me wild
to see you so patient and submissive.

Surangama

Whom are you angry with?

Sudarshana

I do not know; but I wish to see
everything destroyed and convulsed
in ruin and disaster! I left my place
on the throne as the Empress in a

131

moment's time. Did I lose my all to sweep the dust, to sweat and slave in this dismal hole? Why do the torches of mourning not flare up for me all over the world? Why does not the earth quake and tremble? Is my fall but the unobserved dropping of the puny bean-flower? Is it not more like the fall of a glowing star, whose fiery blazon bursts the heavens asunder?

Surangama

A mighty forest inly smokes and smoulders before it bursts into a conflagration: the time has not come yet.

Sudarshana

I have thrown my queen's honour and glory to the dust and winds— but is there no human being who will come out to meet my desolate soul here? Alone—oh, I am fearfully, terribly alone!

Surangama

You are not alone.

Sudarshana

Surangama, I shall not keep anything from you.   When he set the
palace on fire, I could not be angry
with him.   A great inward joy set
my heart a-flutter all the while.   What
a stupendous crime!   What glorious
prowess!   It was this courage that
made me strong and fired my own
spirits.   It was this terrible joy that
enabled me to leave everything behind
me in a moment's time.   But is it all
my imagination only?   Why is there
no sign of his coming anywhere?

Surangama

He of whom you are thinking did
not set fire to the palace—it is the
King of Kanchi who did it.

Sudarshana

Coward! But is it possible? So handsome, so bewitching, and yet no manhood in him! Have I deceived myself for the sake of such a worthless creature? O shame! Fie on me! . . . But, Surangama, don't you think that your King should yet have come to take me back? (SURANGAMA *remains silent*.) You think I am anxious to go back? Never! Even if the King really came I should not have returned. Not even once did he forbid me to come away, and I found all the doors wide open to let me out! And the stony and dusty road over which I walked—it was nothing to it that a queen was treading on it. It is hard and has no feelings, like your King; the meanest beggar is the same to it as the highest Empress. You are silent! Well, I tell you, your King's behaviour is—mean, brutal, shameful!

Surangama

Every one knows that my King is hard and pitiless—no one has ever been able to move him.

Sudarshana

Why do you, then, call him day and night?

Surangama

May he ever remain hard and relentless like rock—may my tears and prayers never move him! Let my sorrows be ever mine only—and may his glory and victory be for ever!

Sudarshana

Surangama, look! A cloud of dust seems to rise over the eastern horizon across the fields.

Surangama

Yes, I see it.

Sudarshana

Is that not like the banner of a chariot?

Surangama

Indeed, a banner it is.

Sudarshana

Then he is coming. He has come at last!

Surangama

Who is coming?

Sudarshana

Our King—who else? How could he live without me? It is a wonder how he could hold out even for these days.

Surangama

No, no, this cannot be the King.

Sudarshana

"No," indeed! As if you know everything! Your King is hard, stony, pitiless, isn't he? Let us see how hard he can be. I knew from the beginning that he would come—that he would have to rush after me. But remember, Surangama, I never for a single moment asked him to come. You will see how I make your King confess his defeat to me! Just go out, Surangama, and let me know everything. (SURANGAMA *goes out*.) But shall I go if he comes and asks me to return with him? Certainly not! I will not go! Never!

Enter SURANGAMA

Surangama

It is not the King, my Queen.

Sudarshana

Not the King? Are you quite sure? What! he has not come yet?

Surangama

No, my King never raises so much dust when he comes. Nobody can know when he comes at all.

Sudarshana

Then this is——

Surangama

The same: he is coming with the King of Kanchi.

Sudarshana

Do you know his name?

Surangama

His name is Suvarna.

Sudarshana

It is he, then. I thought, "I am lying here like waste refuse and offal, which no one cares even to touch." But my hero is coming now to release me. Did you know Suvarna?

Surangama

When I was at my father's home, in the gambling den——

Sudarshana

No, no, I won't hear anything of him from you. He is my own hero, my only salvation. I shall know him without your telling stories about him. But just see, a nice man your King is! He did not care to come to rescue me from even this degradation. You cannot blame me after this. I could not have waited for him all my life here, toiling ignominiously like a bondslave. I shall never have *your* meekness and submissiveness.

XI

Encampment

Kanchi

(*To Kanya Kubja's Messenger.*) Tell
your King that he need not receive
us exactly as his guests. We are
on our way back to our kingdoms,
but we are waiting to rescue Queen
Sudarshana from the servitude and
degradation to which she is condemned
here.

Messenger

Your Highness, you will remember
that the princess is in her father's
house.

Kanchi

A daughter may stay in her father's home only so long as she remains unmarried.

Messenger

But her connections with her father's family remain intact still.

Kanchi

She has abjured all such relations now.

Messenger

Such relationship can never be abjured, Your Highness, on this side of death: it may remain in abeyance at times, but can never be wholly broken up.

Kanchi

If the King chooses not to give up his daughter to me on peaceful terms, our *Kshatriya* code of righteousness will oblige me to employ force. You may take this as my last word.

Messenger

Your Highness, do not forget that our King too is bound by the same code. It is idle to expect that he will deliver up his daughter by merely hearing your threats.

Kanchi

Tell your King that I have come prepared for such an answer.

[MESSENGER *goes out.*

Suvarna

King of Kanchi, it seems to me that we are daring too much.

Kanchi

What pleasure would there be in this adventure if it were otherwise?

Suvarna

It does not cost much courage to challenge Kanya Kubja—but . . .

Kanchi

If you once begin to be afraid of "but," you will hardly find a place in this world safe enough for you.

Enter a SOLDIER

Soldier

Your Highness! I have just received the news that the Kings of Koshala, Avanti, and Kalinga are coming this way with their armies.

[*Exit.*

Kanchi

Just what I was afraid of! The report of Sudarshana's flight has spread abroad—now we are going to be in for a general scramble which is sure to end in smoke.

Suvarna

It is useless now, Your Highness. These are not good tidings. I am perfectly certain that it is our Emperor himself who has secretly spread the report everywhere.

Kanchi

Why, what good will it bring him?

Suvarna

The greedy ones will tear one another to pieces in the general rivalry and scramble—and he will take advantage of the situation to go back with the booty.

Kanchi

Now it becomes clear why your King never shows himself. His trick is to multiply himself on every side— fear makes him visible everywhere. But I will still maintain that your King is but an empty fraud from top to bottom.

Suvarna

But, please Your Highness, will you have the kindness to let me off?

Kanchi

I cannot let you go—I have some use for you in this affair.

Enter a SOLDIER

Soldier

Your Highness, Virat, Panchal, and Vidarbha too have come. They have encamped on the other side of the river.   [*Exit.*

Kanchi

In the beginning we must all fight together. Let the battle with Kanya Kubja first be over, then we shall find some way out of the difficulty.

Suvarna

Please do not drag me into your
plans—I shall be happy if you leave
me alone—I am a poor, mean creature
—nothing can——

Kanchi

Look here, king of hypocrites, ways
and means are never of a very ex-
alted order—roads and stairs and so
forth are always to be trodden under
our feet. The advantage of utilising
men like you in our plans is that we
have to make use of no mask or illusion.
But if I were to consult my prime
minister, it would be absurd for me
to call theft by any name less dignified
than public benefit. I will go now,
and move the princes about like pawns
on the chessboard; the game cannot
evidently go on if all the chessmen
propose moving like kings!

XII

Interior of the Palace

Sudarshana

Is the fight still going on?

Surangama

As fiercely as ever.

Sudarshana

Before going out to the battle my father came to me and said, "You have come away from one King, but you have drawn seven Kings after you: I have a mind to cut you up into seven pieces and distribute them among the princes." It would have been well if he did so. Surangama!

Surangama

Yes?

Sudarshana

If your King had the power to save
me, could my present state have left
him unmoved?

Surangama

My Queen, why do you ask me?
Have I the power to answer for my
King? I know my understanding is
dark; that is why I never dare to
judge him.

Sudarshana

Who have joined in this fight?

Surangama

All the seven princes.

Sudarshana

No one else?

Surangama

Suvarna attempted to escape—in secret before the fight began—but Kanchi has kept him a prisoner in his camps.

Sudarshana

Oh, I should have been dead long ago! But, O King, my King, if you had come and helped my father, your fame would have been none the less! It would have become brighter and higher. Are you quite sure, Surangama, that he has not come?

Surangama

I know nothing for certain.

Sudarshana

But since I came here I have felt suddenly many a time as if somebody were playing on a *vina* below my window.

Surangama

There is nothing impossible in the idea that somebody indulges his taste for music there.

Sudarshana

There is a deep thicket below my window—I try to find out who it is every time I hear the music, but I can see nothing distinctly.

Surangama

Perhaps some wayfarer rests in the shade and plays on the instrument.

Sudarshana

It may be so, but my old window in the palace comes back to my memory. I used to come after dressing in the evening and stand at my window, and out of the blank darkness of our lampless meeting-place used to stream

Doorkeeper

Our King has been taken prisoner.

Sudarshana

Prisoner?   O Mother Earth!

[*Faints.*

XIII

Suvarna

You say, then, that there will be no more necessity of any fight amongst yourselves?

Kanchi

No, you need not be afraid. I have made all the princes agree that he whom the Queen accepts as her husband will have her, and the others will have to abandon all further struggle.

Suvarna

But you must have done with me now, Your Highness—so I beg to be

154

let off now. Unfit as I am for anything, the fear of impending danger
has unnerved me and stunned my
intellect. You will therefore find it
difficult to put me to any use.

Kanchi

You will have to sit there as my
umbrella-holder.

Suvarna

Your servant is ready for anything;
but of what profit will that be to you?

Kanchi

My man, I see that your weak
intellect cannot go with a high ambi-
tion in you. You have no notion yet
with what favour the Queen looked
upon you. After all, she cannot possibly throw the bridal garland on
an umbrella-bearer's neck in a company of princes, and yet, I know, she

will not be able to turn her mind away
from you. So on all accounts this
garland will fall under the shade of
my regal umbrella.

Suvarna

Your Highness, you are entertain-
ing dangerous imaginings about me.
I pray you, please do not implicate
me in the toils of such groundless
notions. I beg Your Highness most
humbly, pray set me at liberty.

Kanchi

As soon as my object is attained,
I shall not keep you one moment from
your liberty. Once the end is attained,
it is futile to burden oneself with the
means.

XIV

SUDARSHANA *and* SURANGAMA *at the Window*

Sudarshana

Must I go to the assembly of the princes, then? Is there no other means of saving father's life?

Surangama

The King of Kanchi has said so.

Sudarshana

Are these the words worthy of a King? Did he say so with his own lips?

157

Surangama

No, his messenger, Suvarna, brought this news.

Sudarshana

Woe, woe is me!

Surangama

And he produced a few withered flowers and said, "Tell your Queen that the drier and more withered these souvenirs of the Spring Festival become, the fresher and more blooming do they grow within in my heart."

Sudarshana

Stop! Tell me no more. Do not torment me any more.

Surangama

Look! There sit all the princes in the great assembly. He who has no ornament on his person, except a single garland of flowers round his crown—he is the King of Kanchi. And he who holds the umbrella over his head, standing behind him—that is Suvarna.

Sudarshana

Is that Suvarna? Are you quite certain?

Surangama

Yes, I know him well.

Sudarshana

Can it be that it is this man that I saw the other day? No, no,—I saw something mingled and transfused and blended with light and darkness, with wind and perfume,—no, no, it cannot be he; that is not he.

Surangama

But every one admits that he is exceedingly beautiful to look at.

Sudarshana

How could *that* beauty fascinate me? Oh, what shall I do to purge my eyes of their pollution?

Surangama

You will have to wash them in that bottomless darkness.

Sudarshana

But tell me, Surangama, why does one make such mistakes?

Surangama

Mistakes are but the preludes to their own destruction.

Messenger (*entering*)

Princess, the Kings are waiting for you in the hall.   [*Exit.*

Sudarshana

Surangama, bring me the veil.

(SURANGAMA *goes out.*) O King, my only King! You have left me alone, and you have been but just in doing so. But will you not know the inmost truth within my soul? (*Taking out a dagger from within her bosom.*) This body of mine has received a stain—I shall make a sacrifice of it to-day in the dust of the hall, before all these princes! But shall I never be able to tell you that I know of no stain of faithlessness within the hidden chambers of my heart? That dark chamber where you would come to meet me lies cold and empty within my bosom to-day—but, O my Lord! none has opened its doors, none has entered it but you, O King! Will you never come again to open those doors? Then, let death come, for it is dark like yourself, and its features are beautiful as yours. It is you—it is yourself, O King!

XV

The Gathering of the PRINCES

Vidarbha

King of Kanchi, how is it that you
have not got a single piece of ornament
on your person?

Kanchi

Because I entertain no hopes at all,
my friend.   Ornaments would but
double the shame of my defeat.

Kalinga

But your umbrella-bearer seems to
have made up for that,—he is loaded
with gold and jewellery all over.

Virat

The King of Kanchi wants to demonstrate the futility and inferiority of outer beauty and grandeur. Vanity of his prowess has made him discard all outer embellishments from his limbs.

Koshala

I am quite up to his trickery; he is seeking to prove his own dignity, maintaining a severe plainness among the bejewelled princes.

Panchala

I cannot commend his wisdom in this matter. Every one knows that a woman's eyes are like a moth in that they fling themselves headlong on the glare and glitter of jewel and gold.

Kalinga

But how long shall we have to wait more?

Kanchi

Do not grow impatient, King of Kalinga—sweet are the fruits of delay.

Kalinga

If I were sure of the fruit I could have endured it. It is because my hopes of tasting the fruit are extremely precarious that my eagerness to have a sight of her breaks through all bounds.

Kanchi

But you are young still—abandoned hope comes back to you again and again like a shameless woman at your age: we, however, have long passed that stage.

Koshala

Kanchi, did you feel as if something shook your seat just now? Is it an earthquake?

Kanchi

Earthquake? I do not know.

Vidarbha

Or perhaps some other prince is coming with his army.

Kalinga

There is nothing against your theory except that we should have first heard the news from some herald or messenger in that case.

Vidarbha

I cannot regard this as a very auspicious omen.

Kanchi

Everything looks inauspicious to the eye of fear.

Vidarbha

I fear none except Fate, before

which courage or heroism is as futile
as it is absurd.

Panchala

Vidarbha, do not darken to-day's
happy proceedings with your unwel-
come prognostications.

Kanchi

I never take the unseen into account
till it has become "seen."

Vidarbha

But then it might be too late to do
anything.

Panchala

Did we not all of us start at a
specially auspicious moment?

Vidarbha

Do you think you insure against
every possible risk by starting at

auspicious moments? It looks as if——

Kanchi

You had better let the "as if" alone: though our own creation, it often proves our ruin and destruction.

Kalinga

Isn't that music somewhere outside?

Panchala

Yes, it sounds like music, sure enough.

Kanchi

Then at last it must be the Queen Sudarshana who is approaching near. (*Aside to* SUVARNA.) Suvarna, you must not hide and cower behind me like that. Mind, the umbrella in your hand is shaking!

Enter GRANDFATHER, *dressed as a warrior*

Kalinga

Who is that?—Who are you?

Panchala

Who is this that dares to enter this hall without being invited?

Virat

Amazing impudence! Kalinga, just prevent the fellow from advancing further.

Kalinga

You are all my superiors in age— you are fitter to do that than myself.

Vidarbha

Let us hear what he has to say.

Grandfather

The KING has come.

Vidarbha (starting)

King?

Panchala

Which King?

Kalinga

Where does he come from?

Grandfather

My King!

Virat

Your King?

Kalinga

Who is he?

Koshala

What do you mean?

Grandfather

You all know whom I mean.   He
has come.

Vidarbha

He has come?

Koshala

With what intention?

Grandfather

He has summoned you all to come to him.

Kanchi

Summoned us, indeed? In what terms has he been pleased to summon us?

Grandfather

You can take his call in any way you like—there is none to prevent you—he is prepared to make all kinds of welcome to suit your various tastes.

Virat

But who are you?

Grandfather

I am one of his generals.

Kanchi

Generals? It is a lie! Do you think
of frightening us? Do you imagine
that I cannot see through your disguise? We all know you well—and
you pose as a "general" before us!

Grandfather

You have recognised me to perfection. Who is so unworthy as I to
bear my King's commands? And yet
it is he who has invested me with these
robes of a general and sent me here:
he has chosen me before greater generals and mightier warriors.

Kanchi

All right, we shall go to observe the
proprieties and amenities on a fitting

occasion—but at present we are in the midst of a pressing engagement. He will have to wait till this little function is over.

Grandfather

When he sends out his call he does not wait.

Koshala

I shall obey his call; I am going at once.

Vidarbha

Kanchi, I cannot agree with you in your proposal to wait till this function is over. I am going.

Kalinga

You are older than I am—I shall follow you.

Panchala

Look behind you, Prince of Kanchi, your regal umbrella is lying in the dust: you have not noticed when your umbrella-holder has stolen away.

Kanchi

All right, general. I too am going— but not to do him homage. I go to fight him on the battle-ground.

Grandfather

You will meet my King in the field of battle: that is no mean place for your reception.

Virat

Look here, friends, perhaps we are all flying before an imagined terror— it looks as if the King of Kanchi will have the best of it.

Panchala

Possibly, when the fruit is so near the hand, it is cowardly and foolish to go away without plucking it.

Kalinga

It is better to join the King of Kanchi. He cannot be without a definite plan and purpose when he is doing and daring so much.

XVI

SUDARSHANA *and* SURANGAMA

Sudarshana

The fight is over now. When will
the King come?

Surangama

I do not know myself: I am also
looking forward to his coming.

Sudarshana

I feel such a throb of joy, Surangama, that my breast is positively
aching. But I am dying with shame
too; how shall I show my face to
him?

Surangama

Go to him in utmost humility and resignation, and all shame will vanish in a moment.

Sudarshana

I cannot help confessing that I have met with my uttermost defeat for all the rest of my life. But pride made me claim the largest share in his love so long. Every one used to say I had such wonderful beauty, such graces and virtues; every one used to say that the King showed unlimited kindness towards me—this is what makes it difficult for me to bend my heart in humility before him.

Surangama

This difficulty, my Queen, will pass off.

Sudarshana

Oh, yes, it will pass—the day has arrived for me to humble myself before the whole world. But why does not the King come to take me back? What more is he waiting for yet?

Surangama

Have I not told you my King is cruel and hard—very hard indeed?

Sudarshana

Go out, Surangama, and bring me news of him.

Surangama

I do not know where I should go to get any news of him. I have asked Grandfather to come; perhaps when he comes we shall hear something from him.

Sudarshana

Alack, my evil fate! I have been reduced to asking others to hear about my own King!

Enter GRANDFATHER

Sudarshana

I have heard that you are my King's friend, so accept my obeisance and give me your blessings.

Grandfather

What are you doing, Queen? I never accept anybody's obeisance. My relation with every one is only that of comradeship.

Sudarshana

Smile on me, then—give me good news. Tell me when the King is coming to take me back.

Grandfather

You ask me a hard question, indeed! I hardly understand yet the ways of my friend. The battle is over, but no one can tell where he is gone.

Sudarshana

Is he gone away, then?

Grandfather

I cannot find any trace of him here.

Sudarshana

Has he gone? And do you call such a person your friend?

Grandfather

That is why he gets people's abuse as well as suspicion. But my King simply does not mind it in the least.

Sudarshana

Has he gone away? Oh, oh, how hard, how cruel, how cruel! He is

made of stone, he is hard as adamant!
I tried to move him with my own
bosom—my breast is torn and bleeding
—but him I could not move an inch!
Grandfather, tell me, how can you
manage with such a friend?

Grandfather

I have known him now—I have
known him through my griefs and
joys—he can make me weep no more
now.

Sudarshana

Will he not let me know him also?

Grandfather

Why, he will, of course. Nothing
else will satisfy him.

Sudarshana

Very well, I shall see how hard he
can be! I shall stay here near the
window without saying a word; I

shall not move an inch; let me see
if he will not come!

Grandfather

You are young still—you can afford
to wait for him; but to me, an old
man, a moment's loss is a week. I
must set out to seek him whether I
succeed or not.   [*Exit.*

Sudarshana

I do not want him—I will not seek
him! Surangama, I have no need of
your King! Why did he fight with
the princes? Was it for me at all?
Did he want to show off his prowess
and strength? Go away from here—
I cannot bear your sight. He has
humbled me to the dust, and is not
satisfied still!

XVII

A Band of Citizens

First Citizen

When so many Kings met together, we thought we were going to have some big fun; but somehow everything took such a turn that nobody knows what happened at all!

Second Citizen

Did you not see, they could not come to an agreement among themselves?—every one distrusted every one else.

Third Citizen

None kept to their original plans; one wanted to advance, another thought it better policy to recede; some went to the right, others made a rush to the left: how can you call that a fight?

First Citizen

They had no eye to real fighting—each had his eye on the others.

Second Citizen

Each was thinking, "Why should I die to enable others to reap the harvest?"

Third Citizen

But you must all admit that Kanchi fought like a real hero.

First Citizen

He for a long time after his defeat seemed loth to acknowledge himself beaten.

Second Citizen

He was at last fixed in the chest by a deadly missile.

Third Citizen

But before that he did not seem to realise that he had been losing ground at every step.

First Citizen

As for the other Kings—well, nobody knows where they fled, leaving poor Kanchi alone in the field.

Second Citizen

But I have heard that he is not dead yet.

Third Citizen

No, the physicians have saved him —but he will carry the mark of his defeat on his breast till his dying day.

First Citizen

None of the other Kings who fled
has escaped; they have all been taken
prisoners.   But what sort of justice is
this that was meted out to them?

Second Citizen

I heard that every one was punished
except Kanchi, whom the judge placed
on his right on the throne of justice,
putting a crown on his head.

Third Citizen

This beats all mystery hollow.

Second Citizen

This sort of justice, to speak frankly,
strikes us as fantastic and capricious.

First Citizen

Just so.   The greatest offender is
certainly the King of Kanchi; as for

the others, greed of gain now pressed them to advance, now they drew back in fear.

Third Citizen

What kind of justice is this, I ask? It is as if the tiger got scot-free, while his tail got cut off.

Second Citizen

If I were the judge, do you think Kanchi would be whole and sound at this hour? There would be nothing left of him altogether.

Third Citizen

They are great, high justices, my friends; their brains are of a different stamp from ours.

First Citizen

Have they got any brains at all, I wonder? They simply indulge their sweet whims as there are none to say anything to them from above.

Second Citizen

Whatever you may say, if we had the governing power in our hands we should certainly have carried on the government much better than this.

Third Citizen

Can there be any real doubts about that? That of course goes without saying.

XVIII

The Street. GRANDFATHER *and* KANCHI

Grandfather
What, Prince of Kanchi, you here!

Kanchi
Your King has sent me on the road.

Grandfather
That is a settled habit with him.

Kanchi
And now, no one can get a glimpse of him.

Grandfather
That too is one of his amusements.

188

Kanchi

But how long more will he elude me like this? When nothing could make me acknowledge him as my King, he came all of a sudden like a terrific tempest—God knows from where—and scattered my men and horses and banners in one wild tumult: but now, when I am seeking the ends of the earth to pay him my humble homage, he is nowhere to be seen.

Grandfather

But however big an Emperor he may be, he has to submit to him that yields. But why have you come out at night, Prince?

Kanchi

I still cannot get rid of the feeling of a secret dread of being laughed at by people when they see me meekly

doing my homage to your King, acknowledging my defeat.

Grandfather

Such indeed is the people. What
would move others to tears only serves
to move their empty laughter.

Kanchi

But you too are on the road, Grandfather.

Grandfather

This is my jolly pilgrimage to the
land of losing everything.

Sings

I am waiting with my all in the hope of
losing everything.
I am watching at the roadside for him
who turns one out into the open
road,

*Who hides himself and sees, who loves
    you unknown to you,*
*I have given my heart in secret love to
    him,*
*I am waiting with my all in the hope
    of losing everything.*

XIX

A Road. SUDARSHANA *and* SURANGAMA

Sudarshana

What a relief, Surangama, what freedom! It is my defeat that has brought me freedom. Oh, what an iron pride was mine! Nothing could move it or soften it. My darkened mind could not in any way be brought to see the plain truth that it was not the King who was to come, it was I who ought to have gone to him. All through yesternight I lay alone on the dusty floor before that window—lay there through the desolate hours and wept! All night the southern winds blew and shrieked and moaned like

192

ceaseless has been my weeping all the way." I shall at least have this pride in me when I meet him.

Surangama

But even that pride will not last. He came before you did—who else could have sent you on the road?

Sudarshana

Perhaps he did. As long as a sense of offended pride remained with me, I could not help thinking that he had left me for good; but when I flung my dignity and pride to the winds and came out on the common streets, then it seemed to me that he too had come out: I have been finding him since the moment I was on the road. I have no misgivings now. All this suffering that I have gone through for his sake, the very bitternesss of all this is giving me his company. Ah!

yes, he has come—he has held me by the hand, just as he used to do in that chamber of darkness, when, at his touch, all my body would start with a sudden thrill: it is the same, the same touch again! Who says that he is not here?—Surangama, can you not see that he has come, in silence and secret? . . . Who is that there? Look, Surangama, there is a third traveller of this dark road at this hour of the night.

Surangama

I see, it is the King of Kanchi, my Queen.

Sudarshana

King of Kanchi!

Surangama

Don't be afraid, my Queen!

Sudarshana

Afraid! Why should I be afraid?
The days of fear are gone for ever for
me.

Kanchi (entering)

Queen-mother, I see you two on this
road! I am a traveller of the same
path as yourself. Have no fear of me,
O Queen!

Sudarshana

It is well, King of Kanchi, that we
should be going together, side by side
—this is but right. I came on your
way when I first left my home, and
now I meet you again on my way back.
Who could have dreamed that this
meeting of ours would augur so well?

Kanchi

But, Queen-mother, it is not meet
that you should walk over this road

on foot.   Will you permit me to get
a chariot for you?

Sudarshana

Oh, do not say so: I shall never be
happy if I could not on my way back
home tread on the dust of the road
that led me away from my King.   I
would be deceiving myself if I were
now to go in a chariot.

Surangama

King, you too are walking in the
dust to-day: this road has never known
anybody driving his horse or chariot
over it.

Sudarshana

When I was the Queen, I stepped
over silver and gold—I shall have
now to atone for the evil fortune of
my birth by walking over dust and

bare earth. I could not have dreamed that thus I would meet my King of common earth and dust at every step of mine to-day.

Surangama

Look, my Queen, there on the eastern horizon comes the dawn. We have not long to walk: I see the spires of the golden turrets of the King's palace.

Enter GRANDFATHER

Grandfather

My child, it is dawn—at last!

Sudarshana

Your benedictions have given me Godspeed, and here I am, at last.

Grandfather

But do you see how ill-mannered our King is? He has sent no chariot, no music band, nothing splendid or grand.

Sudarshana

Nothing grand, did you say? Look, the sky is rosy and crimson from end to end, the air is full of the welcome of the scent of flowers.

Grandfather

Yes, but however cruel our King may be, we cannot seek to emulate him: I cannot help feeling pain at seeing you in this state, my child. How can we bear to see you going to the King's palace attired in this poor and wretched attire? Wait a little— I am running to fetch you your Queen's garments.

Sudarshana

Oh no, no, no! He has taken away those regal robes from me for ever— he has attired me in a servant's dress before the eyes of the whole world: what a relief this has been to me! I am his servant now, no longer his Queen. To-day I stand at the feet of all those who can claim any relationship with him.

Grandfather

But your enemies will laugh at you now: how can you bear their derision?

Sudarshana

Let their laughter and derision be immortal—let them throw dust at me in the streets: this dust will to-day be the powder with which I shall deck myself before meeting my lord.

Grandfather

After this, we shall say nothing. Now let us play the last game of our Spring Festival—instead of the pollen of flowers let the south breeze blow

and scatter dust of lowliness in every
direction! We shall go to the lord
clad in the common grey of the dust.
And we shall find him too covered
with dust all over. For do you think
the people spare him? Even he cannot escape from their soiled and dusty
hands, and he does not even care to
brush the dirt off his garments.

Kanchi

Grandfather, do not forget me in
this game of yours! I also will have
to get this royal garment of mine
soiled till it is beyond all recognition.

Grandfather

That will not take long, my brother.
Now that you have come down so far
—you will change your colour in no
time. Just look at our Queen—she
got into a temper with herself and
thought that she could spoil her match-

less beauty by flinging away all her ornaments: but this insult to her beauty has made it shine forth in tenfold radiance, and now it is in its unadorned perfection.   We hear that our King is all innocent of beauty— that is why he loves all his manifold beauty of form which shines as the very ornament of his breast.   And that beauty has to-day taken off its veil and cloak of pride and vanity!   What could I not give to be allowed to hear the wonderful music and song that has filled my King's palace to-day!

Surangama

Lo, there rises the sun!

XX

The Dark Chamber

Sudarshana

Lord, do not give me back the honour which you once did turn away from me! I am the servant of your feet—I only seek the privilege of serving you.

King

Will you be able to bear me now?

Sudarshana

Oh yes, yes, I shall. Your sigh repelled me because I had sought to find you in the pleasure garden, in my Queen's chambers: there even your meanest servant looks handsomer than you. That fever of longing has left my eyes for ever. You are not beautiful, my lord—you stand beyond all comparisons!

King

That which can be comparable with me lies within yourself.

Sudarshana

If this be so, then that too is beyond comparison. Your love lives in me—you are mirrored in that love, and you see your face reflected in me: nothing of this mine, it is all yours, O lord!

King

I open the doors of this dark room to-day—the game is finished here! Come, come with me now, come outside—*into the light!*

Sudarshana

Before I go, let me bow at the feet of my lord of darkness, my cruel, my terrible, my peerless one!

THE END

THE following pages contain advertisements of books by the same author or on kindred subjects.

BY

RABINDRANATH TAGORE

*Nobel Prizeman in Literature, 1913. Author of "Gitanjali," "The Gardener,"
"The Crescent Moon," "Sadhana."*

Chitra

A Play in One Act

Cloth, 12mo. $1.00 net.

This is a little lyrical drama based upon an incident in
the Mahabharata. In the course of his wanderings in
fulfillment of a vow of penance Arjuna comes to Manipur.
There he sees Chitrangada, the daughter of Chitravahana,
the king of the country. Smitten with her charms, he asks
the king for the hand of his daughter. Out of the king's
reply and the conditions which he imposes upon Arjuna
the story develops. It is a rare bit of idealistic writing,
as beautiful in its thought as it is in expression.

"We did not look for an Oriental even though a seer, to
write a book (especially twenty-five years ago when this
was written) that might serve as example to the most
advanced among modern Occidental women—yet this is
just what Tagore has done. Extended comment upon
Mr. Tagore's play is unnecessary. It is at once as clear
and as profound as a mountain pool." *N. Y. Times.*

PUBLISHED BY

THE MACMILLAN COMPANY

Publishers   64-66 Fifth Avenue   New York

OTHER WORKS BY

RABINDRANATH TAGORE

Nobel Prizeman in Literature, 1913

GITANJALI (Song Offerings). A Collection of Prose Translations made by
the author from the original Bengali $1.50 net
THE GARDENER. Poems of Youth $1.25 net
THE CRESCENT MOON. Child Poems. (Colored Ill.) $1.25 net
SADHANA: THE REALIZATION OF LIFE. A volume of
essays $1.25 net

All four by Rabindranath Tagore, translated by the author from the
original Bengali.

Rabindranath Tagore is the Hindu poet and preacher to whom the Nobel
Prize was recently awarded. . . .

I would commend these volumes, and especially the one entitled "Sadhana," the collection of essays, to all intelligent readers. I know of nothing,
except it be Maeterlinck, in the whole modern range of the literature of the
inner life that can compare with them.

There are no preachers nor writers upon spiritual topics, whether in Europe
or America, that have the depth of insight, the quickness of religious apper-
ception, combined with the intellectual honesty and scientific clearness of
Tagore. . . .

Here is a book from a master, free as the air, with a mind universal as the
sunshine. He writes, of course, from the standpoint of the Hindu. But,
strange to say, his spirit and teaching come nearer to Jesus, as we find Him
in the Gospels, than any modern Christian writer I know.

He does for the average reader what Bergson and Eucken are doing for
scholars; he rescues the soul and its faculties from their enslavement to
logic-chopping. He shows us the way back to Nature and her spiritual
voices.

He rebukes our materialistic, wealth-mad, Western life with the dignity
and authority of one of the old Hebrew prophets. . . .

He opens up the meaning of life. He makes us feel the redeeming fact that
life is tremendous, a worth-while adventure. "Everything has sprung from
immortal life and is vibrating with life. LIFE IS IMMENSE." . . .

Tagore is a great human being. His heart is warm with love. His thoughts
are pure and high as the galaxy.

(Copyright, 1913, by Frank Crane.) Reprinted by permission from the
New York Globe, Dec. 18, 1913.

PUBLISHED BY

THE MACMILLAN COMPANY

Publishers   64-66 Fifth Avenue   New York

Plaster Saints

BY ISRAEL ZANGWILL.   Cloth, 12mo. $1.25 net.

A new play of deep social significance.

The Melting Pot

BY ISRAEL ZANGWILL.   Revised edition.   Cloth, 12mo.

This is a revised edition of what is perhaps Mr. Zangwill's most popular play. Numerous changes have been made in the text, which has been considerably lengthened thereby. The appeal of the drama to the readers of this country is particularly strong, in that it deals with that great social process by which all nationalities are blended together for the making of the real American.

Sword Blades and Poppy Seed

BY AMY LOWELL, Author of "A Dome of Many-Coloured Glass."   Boards, 12mo. $1.25 net.

Of the poets who to-day are doing the interesting and original work, there is no more striking and unique figure than Amy Lowell. The foremost American member of the "Imagists"—a group of poets that includes William Butler Yeats, Ezra Pound, Ford Madox Hueffer—she has won wide recognition for her writing in new and free forms of poetical expression. Miss Lowell's present volume of poems, "Sword Blades and Poppy Seed," is an unusual book. It contains much perhaps that will arouse criticism, but it is a new note in American poetry. Miss Lowell has broken away from academic traditions and written, out of her own time, real singing poetry, free, full of new effects and subtleties.

PUBLISHED BY

THE MACMILLAN COMPANY

Publishers   64–66 Fifth Avenue   New York

Romance

By EDWARD SHELDON, Author of "The Nigger," etc.
Decorated cloth, 12mo.

Mr. Sheldon can be relied upon to provide drama that is not only good from a technical standpoint, but unusual in subject-matter. *The Nigger*, which proved to be one of the sensations of the New Theatre's short career, is now followed by *Romance*, a play more admirable, perhaps, in its construction, and of universal appeal. As a book the story seems to have lost none of its brilliance; in fact the sharpness of its character delineation, the intensity and reality of its plot and the lyrical beauty of some of its passages are, if possible more apparent on the printed page than in the theatre. There is little doubt but that the tremendous success which the drama made when footlighted is to be duplicated upon its appearance in this form.

Poems

By HARRIET MONROE. Cloth, 12mo. $1.25 net.

In this book is brought together some of Miss Monroe's best work. As the editor of *Poetry: A Magazine of Verse*, wherein occasionally compositions of her own have appeared, and as a contributor to the better magazines, Miss Monroe has endeared herself to a large audience of discriminating people. A distinguishing feature of the collection is that it is notably representative of current ideas and sentiments, and pleasingly varied in theme. The author's subjects are chosen from the Panama Canal, the Titanic disaster, the turbine, the telephone, State Street, Chicago, and other modern phases or factors of life. There is also a group of love poems.

PUBLISHED BY

THE MACMILLAN COMPANY

Publishers   64–66 Fifth Avenue   New York

The Congo and Other Poems

BY VACHEL LINDSAY.   Cloth, 12mo.

In the readings which he has given throughout the country Mr. Lindsay has won the approbation of the critics and of his audiences in general for the new verse form which he is employing. The wonderful effects of sound produced by his lines, their relation to the idea which the author seeks to convey and their marvelous lyrical quality are something, it is maintained, quite out of the ordinary and suggest new possibilities and new meanings in poetry. In this book are presented a number of Mr. Lindsay's most daring experiments, that is to say they *were* experiments when they were first tried; they have been more than justified by their reception.   It is believed that the volume will be one of the most discussed of all the year's output.

Earth Triumphant and Other Tales in Verse

BY CONRAD AIKEN.   Cloth, 12mo. $1.25 net.

Conrad Aiken is one of the first American writers to choose to tell his stories in verse. Helston, Masefield and other Europeans have been doing it with marked success, but hitherto this country has had no notable representative in this line of endeavor. Though Mr. Aiken has been writing for a number of years, *Earth Triumphant and Other Tales in Verse* is his first published book. In it are contained, in addition to the several narratives of modern life, a number of shorter lyrics. It is a volume distinguished by originality and power.

PUBLISHED BY

THE MACMILLAN COMPANY

Publishers   64-66 Fifth Avenue   New York

A LIST OF PLAYS

Leonid Andreyev's Anathema . . . . $1.25 net
Clyde Fitch's The Climbers . . . . .75 net
   Girl with the Green Eyes . . . . 1.25 net
   Her Own Way . . . . .75 net
   Stubbornness of Geraldine . . . . .75 net
   The Truth . . . . .75 net
Thomas Hardy's The Dynasts. 3 Parts. Each . . . . . 1.50 net
Henry Arthur Jones's
   Whitewashing of Julia . . . . .75 net
   Saints and Sinners . . . . .75 net
   The Crusaders . . . . .75 net
   Michael and His Lost Angel . . . . .75 net
Jack London's Scorn of Women . . . . 1.25 net
   Theft . . . . 1.25 net
Mackaye's Jean D'Arc . . . . 1.25 net
   Sappho and Phaon . . . . 1.25 net
   Fenris the Wolf . . . . 1.25 net
   Mater . . . . 1.25 net
   Canterbury Pilgrims . . . . 1.25 net
   The Scarecrow . . . . 1.25 net
   A Garland to Sylvia . . . . 1.25 net
John Masefield's The Tragedy of Pompey . . . . 1.25 net
William Vaughn Moody's
   The Faith Healer . . . . 1.25 net
Stephen Phillip's Ulysses . . . . 1.25 net
   The Sin of David . . . . 1.25 net
   Nero . . . . 1.25 net
   Pietro of Siena . . . . 1.00 net
Phillips and Carr. Faust . . . . 1.25 net
Edward Sheldon's The Nigger . . . . 1.25 net
   Romance . . . . 1.25 net
Katrina Trask's In the Vanguard . . . . 1.25 net
Rabindranath Tagore's The Post Office . . . . . . 1.00 net
   Chitra . . . . 1.00 net
   The King of the Dark Chamber . . . . . . 1.25 net
Robinson, Edwin A. Van Zorn . . . . 1.25 net
Sarah King Wiley's Coming of Philibert . . . . 1.25 net
   Alcestis . . . . .75 net
Yeats's Poems and Plays, Vol. II, Revised Edition . . . . . 2.00 net
   Hour Glass (and others) . . . . 1.25 net
   The Green Helmet and Other Poems . . . . . 1.25 net
Yeats and Lady Gregory's Unicorn from the Stars . . . . 1.50 net
Israel Zangwill's The Melting Pot. New Edition . . . 1.25 net
   The War God . . . . 1.25 net
   The Next Religion . . . . 1.25 net
   Plaster Saints . . . . 1.25 net

PUBLISHED BY

THE MACMILLAN COMPANY

Publishers   64-66 Fifth Avenue   New York

DATE DUE

DEMCO 38-297